IMPACT
CALIFORNIA
SOCIAL STUDIES

Weekly Explorer
MAGAZINE

Continuity
and Change

Mc
Graw
Hill
Education

mheducation.com/preK-12

Send all inquiries to:
McGraw-Hill Education
8787 Orion Place
Columbus, OH 43240

ISBN: 978-0-07-899375-6
MHID: 0-07-899375-X

Printed in the United States of America.

1 2 3 4 5 6 QVS 21 20 19 18 17

Explore!

Chapter 1

Communities in California

EQ How does geography impact California communities?

(t)David R. Frazier Photolibrary, Inc./Alamy Stock Photo, (b)powerofforever/Getty Images

Chapter 2

American Indians of the Local Region

 How have California Indians influenced the local region?

(t)Spencer Grant/age fotostock, (c)rab-bit/iStock/Getty Images, (b)photoquest7/iStockphoto/Getty Images

Chapter 3

How and Why Communities Change Over Time

 How has life changed for people in my community over time?

Chapter 4

American Citizens, Symbols, and Government

 How do our government and its citizens work together?

Chapter 5

Economics of the Local Region

Explore!

Welcome to the Weekly Explorer Magazine!

This magazine will give you a chance to explore the world.

- There are articles, songs, stories, and poems for you to read.

- You will look closely at maps, diagrams, infographics, and other images.

- As you read, you will look for answers to an Essential Question (EQ).

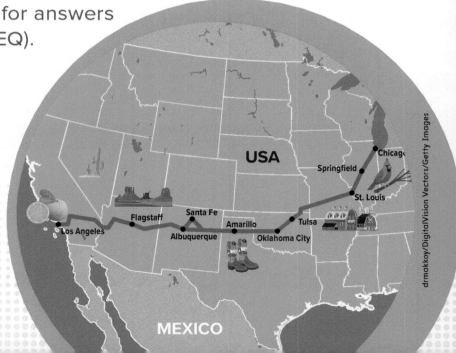

The following steps will help in your exploration.
You can take notes as you read.

1 Inspect

Read the text.

- What does it say?
- What are the details in the images?
- What are the main ideas?

2 Find Evidence

Reread the text and look at the images again.

- Look for more clues about the main ideas.
- What other details do you notice?
- How does the writer support the ideas?
- Be curious!

3 Make Connections

Think about what you've read.

- How does this connect to the EQ?
- How does it connect to other texts?
- How does it connect to you?
- What do you think?

Let's go!

Chapter 1
Communities in California

ESSENTIAL EQ QUESTION

How does geography impact California communities?

Table of Contents

(bkgd)Marco Regalia Sell/Alamy Stock Photo, (t)Mimi Ditchie Photography/Moment Open/Getty Images, (b)Andrei Stanescu/Shutterstock.com

Where Do Californians Live?

California is a big state. It is made up of many different types of land. Our communities are just as varied as our land!

Lake Tahoe is a large freshwater lake surrounded by mountains. People can do lots of outdoor activities here!

The Central Valley region is home to many people. Crops are grown here too, including grapes, peaches, and rice.

San Diego is the second largest city in California. Its warm and sunny climate makes beaches popular places to visit.

Some parts of California have a desert climate. Cacti and other desert plants thrive in these communities.

- What details do you see in the photos?
- What details are similar to where you live?

OUR STATE, OUR FAIR

California State Fair entrance, 1964

Then

Cattle contests have always been held at the California State Fair.

After gold was discovered in California in 1848, many people headed west. California's **population** boomed! California became a state in 1850. Californians wanted to prove that their state was about more than gold—it was also great for farming and industry. The State Agricultural Society decided to plan a fair to showcase their great state.

In 1854, the first California State Fair was held in San Francisco. As many as 15,000 people visited in a single day! Most exhibits were related to farming. People marveled at 2-inch long peanuts, 72-pound beets, and a 10-pound carrot that was 3 feet long. Contests were held to judge livestock.

Over the years, exhibits became more elaborate. Around the turn of the century, fair organizers even staged a full-sized train wreck! It remained a popular attraction until World War I.

People raise and show animals at the fair.

Today's fair includes exhibits about agriculture and new technology. Farmers see DNA profiles of animals they're interested in. The fair is also about having fun. Students enter their best art work and win a prize. Rides and cultural celebrations add to the excitement. There's even a pie-eating contest! More than a million people visit California's state fair each year.

Today, visitors to the fair enjoy fun rides like this one.

Chieko Hara/The Porterville Recorder via AP/AP Images

TO THE FAIR

by Kate Minor

Let's hitch up the buggy
And go to the fair.
We'll see all the people
And animals there.

Ma's packed up some jars
Of her strawberry jam.
Pa wants to see horses
And this year's new lambs.

We might see a strongman
Or maybe a race.
Last year my brother
Ate pie with his face!

So hurry up, family!
Let's get to the fair.
I can't wait to see
All the wonderful there!

WordBlast

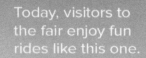

What does the word **population** mean? What clue can you find in the text that helps you know the meaning?

5

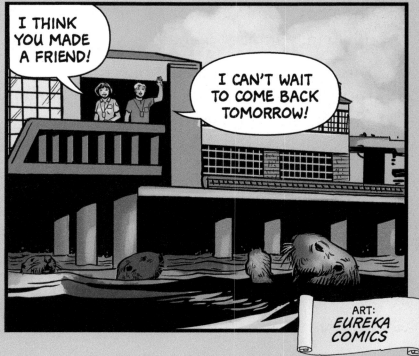

TRASHING THE OCEAN

Imagine floating garbage stretching farther than your eye can see. It stretches from the west coast of North America all the way to Japan. Unfortunately, it's not imaginary. It's real, and it's called the Great Pacific Garbage Patch.

Trash that gets dumped or washed into the ocean floats. Currents of moving water carry the trash along. When multiple currents meet, an area of calm water can form. Once trash lands in the calm water, it stays there, trapped.

You might picture an island of trash. Really, the Patch looks like a lot of soupy water. Why? Because it's made mostly of plastic. Plastic does not ever **decompose**, or rot. It just breaks down into smaller pieces.

These tiny pieces cause huge problems. Turtles mistake plastic for jellies, their favorite food. Seabirds think the plastic is fish eggs. Eating plastic harms and often kills the animals.

So what can we do about the problem? We can limit our use of plastic. We can throw trash away in the right places. We can recycle. And maybe someday we can figure out a way to clean up the Garbage Patch.

WordBlast

What does the word **decompose** mean? How does the text help you figure out the word's meaning?

How You Can Help

Groups work to remove trash from oceans and beaches all around the world. In 2015, nearly 800,000 people picked up more than 18 million pounds of trash!

You can plan your own beach cleanup. Here are a few tips.

☑ Wear heavy work gloves. You will need to protect your hands from anything sharp.

☑ Bring a refillable water bottle filled with fresh water. You can't drink the ocean!

☑ Bring bags and containers to hold what you pick up. Set up a place where you can dispose of the trash.

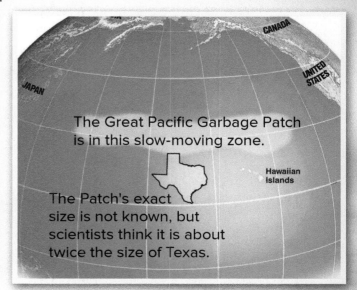

The Great Pacific Garbage Patch is in this slow-moving zone.

The Patch's exact size is not known, but scientists think it is about twice the size of Texas.

Hawaiian Islands

(t)Maschietto/Newscom. (b)Al Seib/Los Angeles Times/Getty Images

JOHN
of the Mountains

John Muir was born in 1838. He was both a woodsman and naturalist. He so loved the outdoors that he devoted his life to preserving it. A sequoia grove, glacier, mountain peak, and lake are all named for Muir.

At age 30, Muir climbed the Sierra Nevada Mountains. He spent the next five years learning about them. He would set off with his blanket roll and a rubber bag containing a little tea, flour, and maybe some oatmeal.

Muir would be gone for days or even weeks. He considered a fifty-mile hike in the rugged mountains a good "two day saunter."

Once he lashed himself to the top of a hundred-foot-high tree during a storm. He wanted to experience how a tree withstands the winds. During another storm, he was trapped overnight. His feet were frostbitten!

But that did not stop Muir from exploring. He learned more about the Sierra Nevada than anyone had ever known. He was the first to realize how glaciers had carved out the valleys.

When he was about fifty years old, Muir started writing articles about the importance of nature. These articles helped convince a group of powerful people to lobby Congress. They supported a bill to **preserve** the Yosemite Valley. Congress passed the Yosemite bill in 1890, creating a national park.

President Theodore Roosevelt was a fan of nature and of Muir's work. He helped pass more laws to protect forests. Roosevelt said that the sequoia trees in California needed protection "simply because it would be a shame to our civilization to let them disappear. They are monuments to themselves."

John Muir and President Theodore Roosevelt visited Yosemite together.

WordBlast

What does it mean to **preserve** something? Tell a partner something you can help to preserve.

"TEXT: Muir, John. My First Summer in the Sierra. Boston, MA: Houghton Mifflin Company, 1911.; PHOTO: (bkgd)©Pgiam/Getty, (t)Library of Congress, Prints and Photographs Division ILC-US262-86721 Images, (b)Russ Bishop/Alamy Stock Photo"

PRIMARY SOURCE

In Their Words...

Now it is plain that the forests are not inexhaustible, and that quick measures must be taken if ruin is to be avoided.

—John Muir

This sign next to Yosemite Creek marks the site of a cabin built by John Muir.

WINTER IN DEATH VALLEY

Late on a winter night in 1849, Juliet Brier walked alone with her three sons. They were in one of the hottest and driest places on Earth. It was the desert of Death Valley. She carried her youngest boys, Kirk and Johnny. Eight-year-old Columbus struggled along in the dark. The trail ahead was faint. James, her husband, trudged far ahead with a few scraggly oxen.

The Briers were part of a large wagon-train company called the Sand Walkers. They started their journey from Salt Lake City, Utah, to the California gold mines in early fall, 1849. In two weeks, people disagreed about which trail to take. The Sand Walkers split up into smaller groups.

This illustration shows the Brier family.

(bkgd)HIT1912/iStockphoto/Getty Images; (inset)boyram/Getty Images

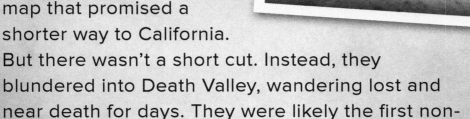

This modern photo shows what the trip across Death Valley might have been like.

The Briers followed behind a small band of about thirty young men called the Jayhawkers. The group followed a map that promised a shorter way to California. But there wasn't a short cut. Instead, they blundered into Death Valley, wandering lost and near death for days. They were likely the first non-native people to enter Death Valley.

Juliet walked slowly with her children. When the Jayhawkers grew weak, they fell back. Juliet acted as a mother to them all. She tended the sick and inspired them to go on. The wagons had to be abandonded. Even though most of the cattle were killed for food, there was not enough. Thirteen men starved. But the Briers lived and carried on.

The group walked through Death Valley and the Mojave Desert to safety in Los Angeles. For many years, the Jayhawkers and the Briers held reunions to share memories of their journey together.

PRIMARY SOURCE

In Their Words...

"Night came down and we lost all track of those ahead. I would search, on my hands and knees, in the starlight for the tracks of the oxen"

— *Juliette Brier*

13

THE HOOVER DAM

SHARING THE WATER

What do a glass of water in Phoenix, a sprinkler in Denver, a toilet in Los Angeles, and a fountain in Las Vegas have in common? It's likely that much of the water in each comes from the same place: the Colorado River.

In the early 1900s many states wanted to claim the river's resources. In 1922, a compact was created. This agreement divided the river's water equally between seven states.

A REALLY BIG DAM

In 1931, work began on the Hoover Dam. It was to be the largest dam in the nation. It was built for a few reasons. It would hold back the Colorado River and prevent flooding. It would help regulate water. Perhaps most importantly, it would provide power through hydroelectric energy.

Hoover Dam

So how big is the Hoover Dam? It is 726 feet tall. That's 171 feet taller than the Washington Monument. Its base is as thick as two football fields laid end to end. The amount of concrete needed to build the dam could make a 4-foot-wide sidewalk all the way around the Earth at the Equator!

AND A HUGE LAKE

When the Hoover Dam was finished and blocked the Colorado River, it created Lake Mead. Lake Mead is a huge **reservoir**. It can hold more water than any reservoir in the United States, enough to cover the entire state of New York in one foot of water. However, Lake Mead hasn't been filled all the way in many years. Drought and the demand for water have kept it at lower levels.

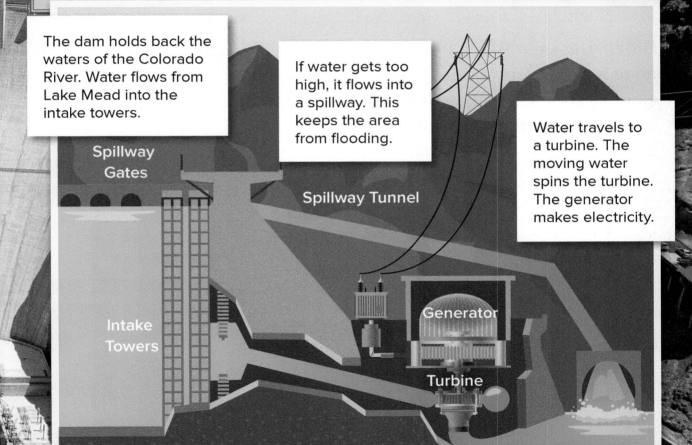

The dam holds back the waters of the Colorado River. Water flows from Lake Mead into the intake towers.

If water gets too high, it flows into a spillway. This keeps the area from flooding.

Water travels to a turbine. The moving water spins the turbine. The generator makes electricity.

Spillway Gates

Spillway Tunnel

Intake Towers

Generator

Turbine

⊕ EXPLORE the InfoGraphic

- How does the Hoover Dam provide power?
- What is the purpose of a spillway?
- Where does the water go after leaving the intake tower?

Your Yard Can Save Water!

Green grass lawns can be pretty, but they need a lot of water to stay alive. Using other kinds of plants in your yard can conserve water. That's good news for places where drought is a problem. Check out these drought-friendly plants.

This desert home is surrounded by plants but not the ones you usually see in yards.

Agave plants store water. They can survive for long periods without rain.

Cacti (the plural of "cactus") can store water AND filter it. They make the water systems around them cleaner.

Sagebrush is native to California. It uses little water and can help prevent erosion.

Take Action!
More to Explore

Here are some ideas for you to think about! You can research and discuss the questions below.

What is special about where you live?

What is Death Valley like today?

What are some other things you can do to save water?

WordBlast

- What caused the **population** of California to grow in the 1800s?

- List two things that **decompose**. List one thing that does not.

- Is it important to **preserve** natural areas? Explain.

- How does a dam create a **reservoir**?

Reflect
How does geography impact California communities?

Chapter 2

AMERICAN INDIANS OF THE LOCAL REGION

ESSENTIAL EQ QUESTION

How have California Indians influenced the local region?

Table of Contents

(t)photoquest7/iStockphoto/Getty Images, (c)rdb-bit/iStock./Getty Images, (bkgd)Eyal Nahmias/Alamy Stock Photo

CONNECTED TO OUR PAST

The California Indians are known as the first people of California. Their ancestors settled the area long before the Europeans came. There are many different groups of California Indians.

A Hupa Indian woman from long ago

Acjachemen Indian girls from today

- What do you notice in the older picture?
- What do you notice in the modern picture?

Sacred Sites

Each group of California Indians has special beliefs. They practice those beliefs at sacred sites. Two of those places are Mount Shasta and Medicine Lake. California Indians perform **traditional** dances and ceremonies at these sites. They gather healing herbs for good health.

MOUNT SHASTA

The Wintu have lived near Mount Shasta for hundreds of years. They believe that their ancestors came from a freshwater spring on the mountain. The spring runs into a beautiful area called Panther Meadows. Every August the Wintu hold sacred ceremonies in the meadows.

Today, many people from around the world visit Mount Shasta. They are drawn to its beauty and awed by its size. However, tourists don't always respect this special place. They place objects in the spring and use too much of its water. They damage plants in the meadows. The Wintu people are working to prevent this in the future to keep their sacred place safe.

Mt. Shasta

WordBlast

What do you think **traditional** means? How does the text help you figure it out?

photoquest7/iStockphoto/Getty Images

Medicine Lake

MEDICINE LAKE

Medicine Lake is not far from Mount Shasta. It is a volcano that has filled with water over time. It is also a sacred place to many California Indians, particularly the Shasta, Modoc, and Pit River groups. These groups believe the lake is a place of great healing. In the lands that overlook the lake, many groups hold traditional ceremonies and gather herbs.

Some companies want to use the lands around Medicine Lake. California Indians are using the law to prevent this. They are working hard to keep their sacred site from harm.

A BIGGER VOICE

AB 52 was a bill that became a law in California in 2015. This law gave California Indians more power to make important decisions about their sacred sites. It also said that the state's public projects could not harm any place or object that was sacred to the Indians.

PRIMARY SOURCE

In Their Words...

Tribes are not formally recognized as ... experts on their cultural and historical resources. This bill will provide certainty to protect these important resources.

—*Mike Gatto, author of Assembly Bill 52*

PHOTO:(t)Richard J. Rauenzahn/Alamy Stock Photo. TEXT:Gatto, Mike. "Assembly Committee on Appropriations." California: April 19, 2013.

The Mighty Redwood

Special Trees

Trees are important natural resources. They provide nuts, fruits, and berries for food. They also supply wood for building. The California coast redwood trees are among the oldest and tallest trees on Earth. They can reach higher than a 30-floor skyscraper. They can also live for more than 2,000 years.

The California Indians of long ago used fallen redwood trees very carefully. Nothing was wasted. They used redwood planks to build their houses. They also used hollowed out logs from redwood trees to build canoes. They traded redwood materials with other tribes.

A California Indian house was understood to be a living being. The redwood used for the walls of a house was thought to be sacred.

GaryKavanagh/iStock/Getty Images

Redwood trees in California

Saving the Redwoods

As California grew in the 1800s, people needed lumber to build houses. They looked at the giant redwoods and saw just what they needed. The great trees were cut down and milled into boards. Soon, only a few stands of redwoods were left. People realized they had to protect the giant, ancient trees. They formed a group to protect the trees by buying land and making parks where the trees could not be cut down.

California Big Trees: A Paiute Legend

The Paiute Indians called the redwood trees *woh-woh-nau*. Say those sounds out loud. Do you sound like a bird? The Paiute word **mimics** an owl's hoot. The Paiute believed the redwood trees were watched over by owls. Cutting down a redwood tree or hurting an owl was thought to bring bad luck.

WordBlast

If you **mimic** something, what are you doing?

POWWOW POWER

The term *powwow* comes from the American Indian word *pauwau*. Long ago, a powwow was a healing ceremony. It was led by a medicine man. American Indians held the ceremonies to celebrate and give thanks for a successful hunt.

Today, powwows are joyful social gatherings. Special clothes called **regalia** are worn at powwows. The clothes can be decorated with beads, feathers, ribbon, and yarn.

Powwows include drumming, singing, and dancing. They also can include handmade crafts and traditional foods like buffalo meat or acorn soup. You can find powwows all across the United States.

WordBlast

What is **regalia**? What kinds of decorations are used to make regalia?

(bkgd:Aurum/Alamy Stock Photo)

Families celebrate together at powwows.

THE POWERFUL DRUM

The drum is an important part of the powwow. It is treated with respect. American Indians say the drum brings the heartbeat of the Earth Mother to the powwow for all to hear and feel. Drums set the rhythm for the dances that happen in a circle. Everyone sits around the drum and hits the drum at the same time. The sound is very loud and powerful. It creates a beat that encourages singing and dancing.

Many dances are performed at powows.

CELEBRATING ACORNS

Did you know that people can eat acorns? It's true! For thousands of years, acorns were an important food source for many California Indians. The Miwok are one group that relied on acorns. Each fall, the Miwok gathered acorns. They ground the nuts into powder. Then they used the acorn powder to make bread, biscuits, and soup.

Today, acorns are not a big part of any group's diet. However, California Indians and others still celebrate and honor the acorn at the Miwok Acorn Festival near Sacramento.

This two-day festival is held every year on the last weekend in September. Different groups gather to make and eat foods made from acorns. They also perform traditional dances, play games, and tell stories.

Miwok women ground acorns. Then they sifted the powder in baskets.

(bkgd)rab-bit/iStock/Getty Images, (l)George Ostertag/age fotostock/SuperStock, (r)Buyenlarge/Archive Photos/Getty Images

HOW TO ROAST ACORNS FOR EATING

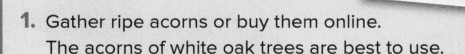

With the help of an adult, follow these steps to roast acorns.

1. Gather ripe acorns or buy them online. The acorns of white oak trees are best to use.

2. Shell the acorns. Crack them using a nutcracker. Put them in a pot of boiling water. Boil them for about 15 minutes. Change the water and boil them again until the water is no longer brown. This removes the bitter taste.

3. Preheat the oven to 350°F. Rinse and spread the acorns on clean towels to dry. Then, spread them on a baking sheet and place the baking sheet in the oven.

4. Roast the acorns for one hour. After the acorns cool, enjoy them on salads, in stews, or as a tasty topping for oatmeal.

 EXPLORE the InfoGraphic

- How do you get rid of the bitter taste of acorns?
- How long should you roast the acorns?
- What are the best kind of acorns to use?

READY TO DANCE

American Indians call the outfits they wear when dancing at powwows *REGALIA*. They never call them costumes.

HEY DENA, WHAT DO YOU THINK OF MY REGALIA?

YOU LOOK GREAT! YOU'RE READY FOR THE GRASS DANCE.

Long ago, it is said, young boys were sent out to flatten the grass before a celebration. This motion turned into a dance.

I HELPED MY MOM SEW THE FRINGE ON.

YOU SHOULD GET DRESSED, TOO. WE'LL BE DANCING SOON.

Metal cones are sewn on the dresses for the jingle dress dance.

I CAN'T! LOOK! MOM DIDN'T NOTICE SOME CONES ARE MISSING.

EVERYONE'S REGALIA WILL BE PERFECT EXCEPT MINE.

WHERE IS YOUR MOM?

SHE LEFT EARLY TO PRACTICE HER BUCKSKIN DANCE.

The buckskin dance is one of the oldest dances. It is a beautiful dance that involves a lot of practice and skill.

YOU DON'T HAVE MUCH TIME. WE BETTER GET THOSE CONES SEWN ON.

I DON'T KNOW HOW TO SEW!

I DO! LET'S GET TO WORK!

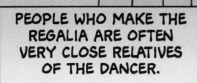

PEOPLE WHO MAKE THE REGALIA ARE OFTEN VERY CLOSE RELATIVES OF THE DANCER.

WHO MADE THIS DRESS, DENA?

MY GRANDMOTHER.

IT LOOKS PERFECT! THANKS, PETE!

I HEAR THE DRUM!

WE BETTER RUN!

ART: EUREKA COMICS

AMERICAN INDIAN RODEOS

What do you think of when you picture cowboys and cowgirls? You probably see people in cowboy hats riding horses and swinging ropes. And you would be right!

The tradition of cowboys and cowgirls goes back to the early days of cattle ranching. Spanish settlers brought horses and cattle to Southern California. California Indians living in the area learned how to use horses to herd cattle.

It soon became a way of life for the American Indian cowboys and cowgirls.

Today, the tradition continues in the form of **rodeo**. Every weekend, American Indian cowgirls compete in barrel races. American Indian cowboys participate in bronco and bull riding. These competitions require a lot of skill and practice. They are a time-honored tradition for many American Indians.

WordBlast

What do you think a **rodeo** is? What words in the last paragraph help you figure out its meaning?

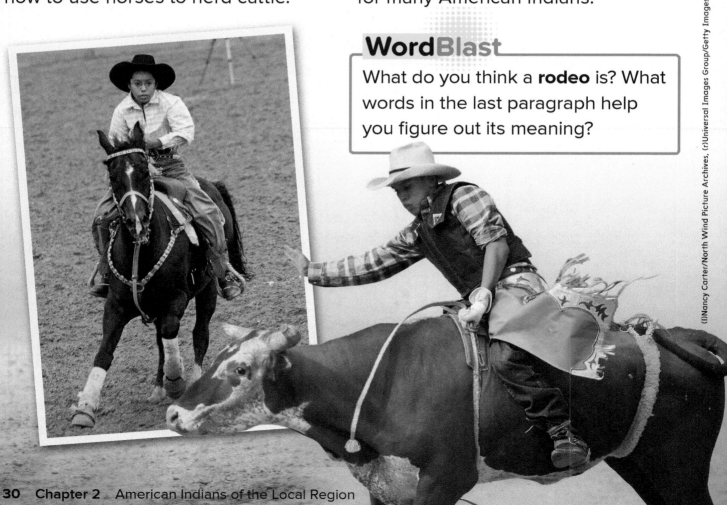

(l)Nancy Carter/North Wind Picture Archives, (r)Universal Images Group/Getty Images

Take Action!

More to Explore

What else do you want to know? The questions below have more ideas that you can research and discuss.

What other California Indian traditions would you like to learn about?

Where can you see redwood trees?

What are some ways to help keep sacred sites safe?

Word Blast

- How does the Paiute word for redwood **mimic** a sound in nature?

- What kinds of **regalia** are worn at powwows?

- What might you see at a **rodeo** today?

- What makes ceremonies at Medicine Lake **traditional**?

Reflect
How have California Indians influenced the local region?

Chapter 3

How and Why Communities Change Over Time

ESSENTIAL EQ QUESTION

How has life changed for people in my community over time?

Table of Contents

(t)Digiphoto/iStock/Getty Images, (bl)i love images/Juice Images/Getty Images, (bkgd)bayram/E+/Getty Images

A Neighborhood Changes

The first Chinese immigrants came to San Francisco in 1848. They built a community in the center of the city. Chinatown became a busy neighborhood.

Today, Chinatown is still busy. Shops, restaurants, and activities draw visitors from around the world.

What is different about the two photographs? What is the same?

GOLD!

In 1848, gold was discovered in the hills of California. One year later, the Gold Rush was on! California became a **destination** for people looking for riches. They came by wagons from the eastern United States, Canada, and Mexico. Others came from places such as China and Chile by boat. Miners settled in central California and in cities like San Francisco.

WordBlast

What do you think a **destination** is? Check your answer in the Glossary.

People came from all over the world to find gold in California.

A CHANGING WAY OF LIFE

The Maidu Indians lived in the Sierra Nevada where gold was discovered. Their home was quickly overrun by miners with gold fever. Many of the Maidu and other California Indians had to go to work in the mines as their lands disappeared. Miners and settlers took their land and changed their way of life forever.

WOMEN OF THE GOLD RUSH

Most gold prospectors were men, but women were also part of the Gold Rush. Some came west with their families or husbands. Some brave fortune seekers came to California on their own. Women discovered that they could make a living. Prospectors paid women to cook for them. Women also ran hotels.

Women played an important role in the Gold Rush.

NEAR AND FAR

Miners came from near and far. African Americans hoped to start a new life. In many cases, they also hoped to earn their freedom. Other men came from China. They worked hard to earn money and build a new life. They were not always paid fairly. Gold seekers from Chile and Mexico faced similar challenges.

Chinese gold rush miners

(t)North Wind Picture Archives/Alamy Stock Photo, (b)Hulton Archive/Archive Photos/Getty Images

PAVING THE WAY WEST

ROUTE US 66

US Highway 66, also called Route 66, was a famous highway. It was built in the 1920s, when the idea of highways—and cars—was still new. The road ran from Chicago to Los Angeles.

In the 1930s, thousands of people followed Route 66 as they moved west to escape the Dust Bowl. The road was not even completely paved. But it was still seen as the way to a better life.

In the 1940s during World War II, the government used the highway to move troops and equipment. After the war, gas stations, hotels, and restaurants opened all along the road. More people used the highway to move to California. California cities grew.

By the early 1980s, new modern highways had been built in place of Route 66. Today, there are still historic signs and museums along the old route. Route 66 helped **transform** the towns and cities along its path. It helped change and shape the country from the Midwest to California.

WordBlast

What do you think the word **transform** means? How do you know?

of America

Pasadena

Angeles   San Bernardino

CANADA

USA

Chicago

Springfield

St. Louis

Flagstaff

Santa Fe

Amarillo

Tulsa

Albuquerque

Oklahoma City

Los Angeles

MEXICO

✴ EXPLORE the Map!

Look closely at the map.

- Route 66 ran from Chicago to Los Angeles. List three other cities it went through.
- What are three states Route 66 went through?
- Could you get from Colorado to California on Route 66?

California

GET YOUR KICKS ON ROUTE 66

The Dust Bowl Migration

MANY TRAVEL WEST. SOME WALK AND SOME DRIVE.

WHERE ARE WE GOING?

WELL, I'VE HEARD GOOD THINGS ABOUT CALIFORNIA.

AT NIGHT, THEY CAMP IN TENTS OR SLEEP UNDER THE STARS.

THE GROUND IS AWFULLY LUMPY.

JUST MAKE SURE NONE OF THE LUMPS ARE SNAKES.

IF A CAR BREAKS DOWN, IT'S HARD TO GET PARTS TO FIX IT.

I HOPE THE BRAKES WILL WORK IN THE MOUNTAINS.

I HOPE THE PATCH ON THIS TIRE WILL LAST.

BUT WHAT AWAITS THEM IN CALIFORNIA IS NOT WHAT EVERYONE EXPECTS.

THIS JOB ONLY PAYS 20 CENTS AN HOUR!

THAT'S BETTER THAN STARVING.

SOME PEOPLE ARE STILL HOMELESS.

BUT WE CAN'T GO BACK. THERE'S NOTHING TO GO BACK TO.

YEARS PASS BEFORE MANY OF THE MIGRANTS TRULY SETTLE DOWN.

LIFE WAS HARD UNTIL WE FINALLY GOT OUR OWN HOUSE.

AT LAST CALIFORNIA FEELS LIKE HOME.

TEXT: *STEPHEN KRENSKY*
ART: *EUREKA COMICS*

It's Dry Out There

A drought is a long period when there is not enough rain. In California, drought can be a serious problem. With little rain, fire danger increases. One spark in a dry area can start a fire. Once a fire starts, it can spread quickly. Wildfires can be big and scary, especially near homes. To **prevent** the spread of fires, new homes are built with materials that don't burn easily. Taking out dead plants and trees can also be a big help.

WordBlast

When you **prevent** something, what do you do? Look for clues in the paragraph.

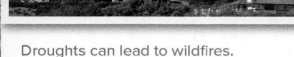

Droughts can lead to wildfires.

Fire Watchers Keep California Safe

To help prevent wildfires, the National Parks hire fire lookouts. The lookouts sit in watchtowers high above the trees looking below for any signs of fire. They must stay awake and alert so they don't miss a fire starting. When they see a fire, they call firefighters. Firefighters come and extinguish the blaze before it gets out of control. These fire watchers help protect the parks and all of us from wildfires.

HOORAY FOR HOLLYWOOD

Hollywood is a neighborhood in Los Angeles, California. It is known as the home of the movie business in the U.S. The movie-making business helped turn Los Angeles into a big city.

People called studio heads were in charge at the movie studios. They made actors into big stars. Shirley Temple was one of the biggest stars in the 1930s. She made her first Hollywood movie when she was only 6 years old! The little girl cheered up movie-goers during the Great Depression.

Shirley Temple

(t) Bettmann/Getty Images, (bt)Time Life Pictures/ The LIFE Picture Collection/Getty Images, (bkgd) Bettmann/Getty Images

Mark Bassett / Alamy Stock Photo

Today, movie-making is still a big **industry** in Los Angeles. Those early studio heads would be surprised to see a movie today. Special effects make amazing worlds come to life. We still have real actors, but we also have computer-drawn ones!

WordBlast

What do you think **industry** means? Look at the other paragraphs for clues.

Strawberry Season

Tiempo de fresa

by Guadalupe Lopez

Warm sunny days	Cálidos días de sol
Cool foggy nights	Noches de niebla
Summer on the Central Coast	Verano en la Costa Central
Strawberry season is here!	Es tiempo de la fresa
Sweet ruby hearts	Dulce fruta corazón
in fields of green	sobre manta verde
Pick now while ripe	Hay que pizcarlas hoy
For tomorrow they are gone	Pues mañana ya no hay

Take Action!

More to Explore

What else do you want to know about? Here are some questions that you can research and discuss.

How has your neighborhood changed? How can you find out?

Which places along old Route 66 would you like to visit?

Other than gold, what brought people to California?

WordBlast

- Why was California a **destination** for so many immigrants in the 1840s?

- How did the movie **industry** change Los Angeles?

- Why is it important to **prevent** wildfires?

- How did Route 66 help **transform** California?

Reflect

How has life changed for people in my community over time?

Chapter 4

American Citizens, Symbols, and Government

How do our government and its citizens work together?

Table of Contents

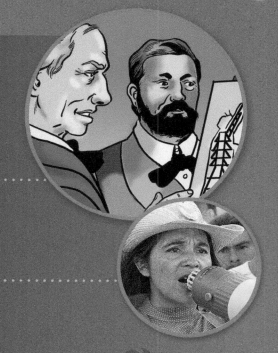

(cl)©1976 George Ballis/Take Stock/The Image Works, (bkgd)TongRo Image Stock/Alamy Stock Photo

CELEBRATE OUR SYMBOLS

GABRIELLE LURIE/AFP/Getty Images

Our state and national symbols stand for things we are proud of. What California symbols do you see? What United States symbols do you see?

The Story Of The Statue Of Liberty

IN 1865, EDOUARD DE LABOULAYE HAS AN IDEA. HE HIRES FRÉDÉRIC-AUGUSTE BARTHOLDI TO SCULPT A MONUMENTAL STATUE.

IT WILL REPRESENT THE FRIENDSHIP BETWEEN FRANCE AND THE UNITED STATES.

AND THE IDEAL OF FREEDOM ITSELF.

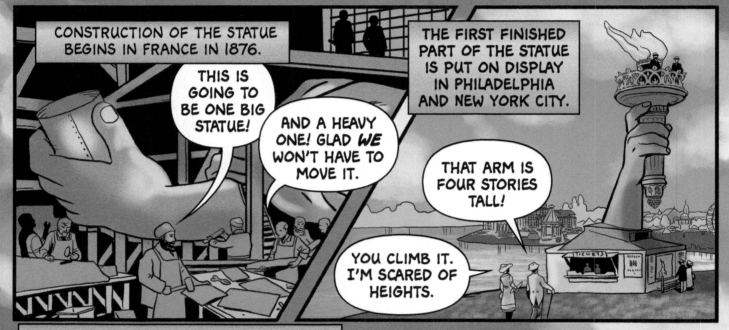

CONSTRUCTION OF THE STATUE BEGINS IN FRANCE IN 1876.

THIS IS GOING TO BE ONE BIG STATUE!

AND A HEAVY ONE! GLAD *WE* WON'T HAVE TO MOVE IT.

THE FIRST FINISHED PART OF THE STATUE IS PUT ON DISPLAY IN PHILADELPHIA AND NEW YORK CITY.

THAT ARM IS FOUR STORIES TALL!

YOU CLIMB IT. I'M SCARED OF HEIGHTS.

IN 1881, BARTHOLDI CALLS ON GUSTAVE EIFFEL, THE MAN WHO WILL LATER BUILD THE EIFFEL TOWER, TO FINISH THE STATUE.

IT WILL BE MADE OF COPPER, AND COPPER NEEDS SUPPORT.

I WILL MAKE A FLEXIBLE SYSTEM, LIKE A SKELETON.

THE YEAR IS 1885. THE STATUE OF LIBERTY ARRIVES IN NEW YORK HARBOR. MANY PEOPLE COME FOR THIS HISTORIC LANDING.

SO SHE'S HEADED OUT TO BEDLOE'S ISLAND.

YOU'LL BE ABLE TO SEE HER FROM ANYWHERE IN THE HARBOR!

DESIGNED BY AMERICAN RICHARD MORRIS HUNT, THE PEDESTAL TO HOLD THE STATUE IS FINISHED IN 1886.

ART: EUREKA COMICS

FIRST, BUILDERS ATTACH THE STATUE'S SKELETON. IT IS MADE OF IRON.

THEN, THE COPPER PLATES ARE ATTACHED TO THE FRAME. IT TAKES FOUR MONTHS TO PUT ALL THE PIECES TOGETHER.

AS YEARS PASS, THE COPPER WILL TURN GREEN FROM EXPOSURE TO AIR.

THE STATUE IS DEDICATED ON OCTOBER 28, 1886. A POEM BY EMMA LAZARUS IS ADDED TO THE BASE IN 1903. TODAY, MORE THAN FOUR MILLION PEOPLE VISIT THE STATUE EACH YEAR.

49

AN UNFAIR LAW

This illustration shows what Chinese workers in California looked like in the 1800s.

The United States is a country filled with people from other places. During the 1800s, many immigrants came to California from China. They worked in the gold fields, in factories, and on the railroads. However, some Americans wanted to stop people moving to the United States from China. They were afraid Chinese workers would take too many jobs.

In 1882, a law called the Chinese Exclusion Act was passed. When you **exclude** something, you do not let it in. The law stopped almost all Chinese immigration for ten years. It also made it hard for Chinese people already in the United States to leave and come back. Then, after ten years had gone by, the law was passed again. This time, it did not have an end date.

The law was not fair, but it stayed in place for many years. Finally, in 1943, President Franklin D. Roosevelt called the law a "historic mistake." He helped to make the law less strict. However, it was not fully **repealed** until 1965.

WordBlast

What word means the opposite of **exclude**?

WordBlast

The word *repeal* comes from an old French word that means "to call back." What do you think happens when a law is **repealed**?

LIFE ON ANGEL ISLAND

Angel Island is near the coast of San Francisco. It became an immigration center in 1910. Most Chinese immigrants had to pass through the island to enter the United States. It was often the hardest part of the journey. Men were separated from women and children. Everyone had to be tested for illness. People sometimes waited weeks or months before they could come into the United States.

The photographs show Chinese immigrants arriving at Angel Island.

SPEAKING WITH SEVEN TONGUES

Dolores Huerta grew up in Stockton, California in the 1930s. She and her brothers lived with their mother and grandfather. Dolores learned to speak her mind early in life. In fact, her grandfather called her "seven tongues" because she talked so much—and so well.

When Dolores was a child, the United States was struggling through the Great Depression. Many of her neighbors were farm workers. They moved from place to place to pick the ripe crops. They were hired for short periods of time. They worked very long hours and were paid very little money. Dolores saw how hard their lives were.

Migrant farm workers in the 1930s

After World War II, Dolores' mother ran a small hotel. She often let the farm workers stay there for free. Dolores learned about fairness and kindness from her mother. Dolores did not see her father very often, but she learned from him, too. He worked as a miner and as a farm worker. He showed Dolores that she could work to change things she didn't like.

Growing up around farm workers led Dolores to want to help others. She wanted to be a voice for change. As an adult, Dolores became an **activist**. She used her voice and her skills to fight for the rights of farm workers. She and her friend César Chávez started the Farm Workers Association to do just that.

It took several years, but their efforts made a big difference. The farm workers were able to ask for better wages and working hours. Dolores didn't stop there. She kept fighting for others, and she is still working and speaking.

Dolores Huerta uses her "seven tongues" to speak for those in need. She continues to work hard to help others today.

WordBlast

What does an **activist** do?

Dolores Huerta is still an activist today.

Dolores Huerta has spoken out for many years.

(l)©1976 George Ballis/Take Stock/The Image Works, (r)REUTERS/Alamy Stock Photo

DISASTER!

THE NATIONAL GUARD

Whom are you going to call if there's an earthquake, a hurricane, or a forest fire? Whatever the disaster, the National Guard is there to help!

The National Guard is a reserve military force for the United States. Their purpose is to be ready to protect and help Americans in an emergency. If there is a natural disaster, the governor of a state can call out the National Guard units.

A Guard soldier must be ready for anything. When tornadoes strike, Guard soldiers are sent out to clear fallen trees and other **debris**. When an area floods, the Guard might use boats to search for people who are trapped. They bring victims to shelters. They provide cots and blankets for people in need. And they don't just rescue people! One group, the Louisiana National Guard, has rescued more than 1,400 pets.

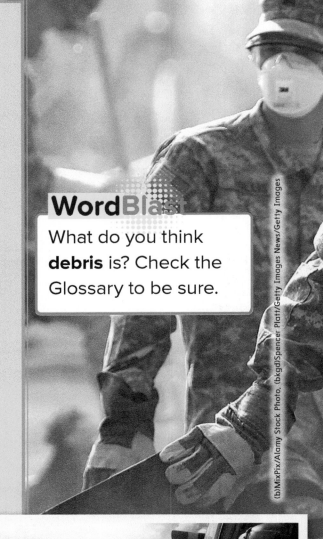

WordBlast
What do you think **debris** is? Check the Glossary to be sure.

(b)MixPix/Alamy Stock Photo, (bkgd)Spencer Platt/Getty Images News/Getty Images

A National Guard soldier views a forest fire from above.

EXPLORE the Map

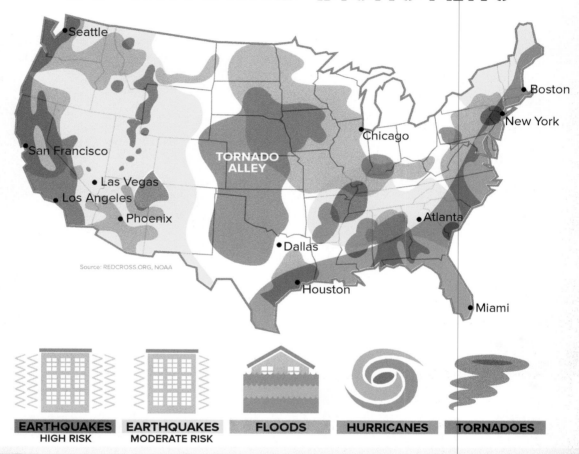

US NATURAL DISASTERS

Seattle

San Francisco

Las Vegas

Los Angeles

Phoenix

TORNADO ALLEY

Dallas

Houston

Chicago

Atlanta

Boston

New York

Miami

Source: REDCROSS.ORG, NOAA

| EARTHQUAKES HIGH RISK | EARTHQUAKES MODERATE RISK | FLOODS | HURRICANES | TORNADOES |

Use the map to answer the questions.

- On which coast are earthquakes more likely to happen?
- What does the orange color on the map show?
- What kind of disaster would the National Guard likely help with in Oklahoma?
- If you lived in Miami, what might you need to prepare for?

Welcome, New Friends

First Daughters

Every four years, the United States elects a president. Sometimes we vote to keep the same person for four more years. Sometimes we vote for a new person. But every time a new president takes office, the same thing happens. One family moves out of the White House and another family moves in.

Jenna Bush Hager and Barbara Bush are twins. They were teenagers when their father, George W. Bush, was elected president in 2000. The twins lived in the White House for eight years.

A new president named Barack Obama won the office in 2008. It was time for the Bush family to leave the White House. President Bush wrote a letter welcoming the new president. The Bush

twins also wrote a letter. Their letter went to President Obama's daughters, Sasha and Malia.

In the letter, the Bush daughters gave Sasha and Malia some good advice. They told the 7- and 10-year-old girls to have fun. They said it was okay to slide down the bannisters. They told them to play on the White House lawn and have pets. They also said it was important for the girls to keep their good and loyal friends.

The Bush daughters didn't have to write a letter. But they wanted to help. They wanted to make the White House feel like a home for two little girls. And when the Obamas left the White House in 2017, the Bushes wrote them a new letter. It said welcome back to the "real" world!

Inviting the Bears

A Retelling of a Tlingit Folktale

There was once an old man who was alone in the world. One day, the man saw two huge grizzly bears fishing in a stream. The bears snorted and growled when they saw the man.

But the man hid his fear. "Hello, great Grizzlies. I have no friends or family to share my table. Please come and feast with me this evening."

The bears looked at him quietly, and nodded. The man rushed home to prepare for his guests. That evening he served the bears a great feast. After the meal, the largest bear turned to him. "I too have lost family and friends. The bears will always be your friends."

To this day, the Tlingit make friends by feasting together.

THAT BECAME A LAW?

Most laws make sense when you think about them. Buckle your seat belt. Do not litter. However, there are some laws that don't make a whole lot of sense today. Or maybe they never quite did!

ARIZONA: Even if your barn is full, it's against the law to let your donkey sleep in the bathtub.

MINNESOTA: It is illegal to eat hamburgers on Sunday in St. Cloud, Minnesota. Better get your burgers on another day!

NEVADA: It is illegal to drive a camel on the highway. Find another way to cross the desert!

WASHINGTON: You may not chase or bother Bigfoot, Sasquatch, or any other undiscovered animal. (Hopefully, they won't chase you either!)

Take Action!
More to Explore

Here are some ideas for you to think about!

What are some laws that you think are fair? What are some laws you think are unfair?

Who are some other people working to make changes today?

What other groups help people during and after disasters?

WordBlast

- What is something an **activist** might do?

- Why is **debris** a problem after a natural disaster?

- If you **exclude** someone from a game, how does that person feel? Why?

- How do you think the **repeal** of the Chinese Exclusion Act might have changed lives?

ESSENTIAL EQ QUESTION

Reflect
How do our government and its citizens work together?

Chapter 5

ECONOMICS
of the LOCAL REGION

How do people in a community meet their needs?

Table of Contents

(t)Ron_Thomas/E+/Getty Images; (b)Tina Stallard/The Image Bank/Getty Images; (bkgd)Kit_Leong/iStock/Getty Images

CALIFORNIA CROPS

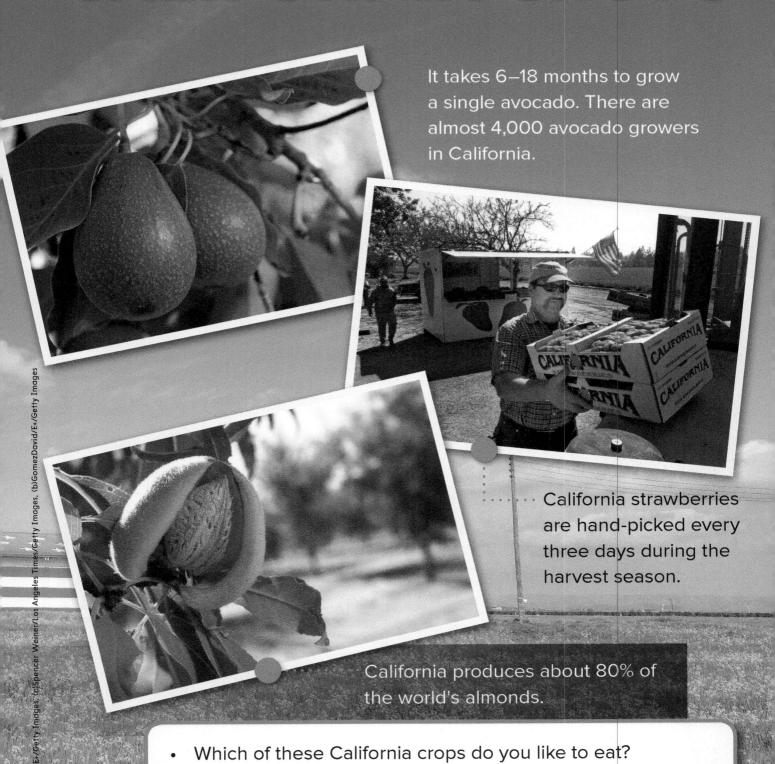

It takes 6–18 months to grow a single avocado. There are almost 4,000 avocado growers in California.

California strawberries are hand-picked every three days during the harvest season.

California produces about 80% of the world's almonds.

- Which of these California crops do you like to eat?
- Why do you think California is able to grow so many crops?

(tl)GomezDavid/E+/Getty Images, (b)Spencer Weiner/Los Angeles Times/Getty Images, (tr)GomezDavid/E+/Getty Images

POWERING THE FUTURE

Much of the energy we use comes from fossil fuels. These are things like coal, oil, and natural gas. Once the fuels are used up, they will be gone forever. The good news is that there are other **sources** of energy that will NEVER run out.

Solar power uses the energy of the sun. Special panels collect energy from the sun's rays. That energy is turned into electricity for homes and businesses.

Wind power is—can you guess? Yes! It is energy made using the wind. Giant wind turbines have blades that turn in the wind. The blades spin a generator. The generator makes electricity.

A sunny, windy day can be pretty POWERFUL!

WordBlast

What do you think the word **source** means? Check the Glossary to be sure.

There are more than 13,000 wind turbines in California.

California produces more solar power than any other state.

MAKE A SOLAR PIZZA BOX OVEN

You can harness the power of the sun. Ask an adult to help you.

Materials: large cardboard pizza box, scissors, aluminum foil, tape, glue, plastic wrap, black construction paper, ruler.

Directions:

1. On the top of the pizza box lid, draw a square. It should be about one inch in from each side of the box. Use scissors to cut along THREE sides to make a big flap. Fold the flap up. It should stand up when the box lid is closed.

2. Cover the inside of the flap with foil, shiny side up. Use tape to hold it in place.

3. Put foil on the inside bottom of the box and glue it in place.

4. Glue black construction paper over the top of the foil in the box.

5. Stretch plastic wrap across the hole in the lid. Glue or tape it in place.

6. Place the solar oven on a flat surface in bright sunlight.

7. Place food you want to heat on a plate. (Tortillas with cheese work well!) Put the plate in the oven.

8. Prop the flap open with a ruler. Turn the box so that the flap reflects sunlight right onto the food.

9. Wait for your treat to heat. It should take about 30–45 minutes. Turn the box as needed so the flap faces the sun. Enjoy!

Have you eaten a juicy, ripe peach? Tasted wildflower honey? Do you like fresh bread? The place you need to go is a farmers' market! There is so much to see and even more to taste. And it all comes from right around where you live!

California has more than 700 farmers' markets. That's more than any other state. The markets are fun, and they have the freshest foods. Farmers' markets are also good for farmers. They can sell their **produce** close to home.

WordBlast

The word **produce** has more than one meaning. What does it mean in the article?

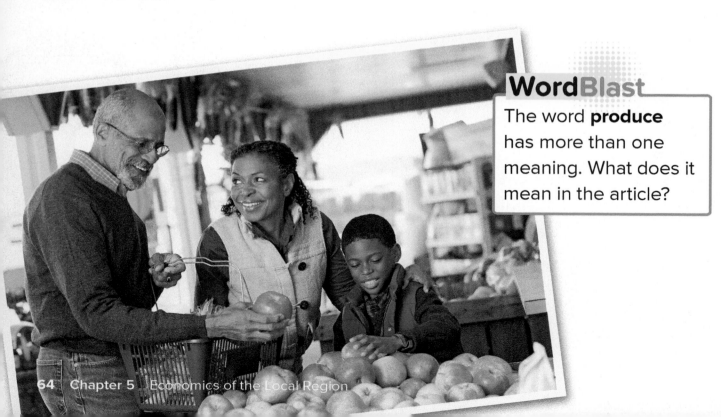

SUPPORT YOUR FARMER!

Farmers' markets aren't the only way to support farmers in your area. You can also ask your family to join a CSA. CSA stands for Community Supported Agriculture. In a CSA, people buy straight from a farmer. They pay the farmer, and the farmer delivers boxes of fresh produce right to their door.

Check out a farmers' market near you. Sign up for a CSA. You might find some new favorite foods!

You can have a box of vegetables delivered to your home.

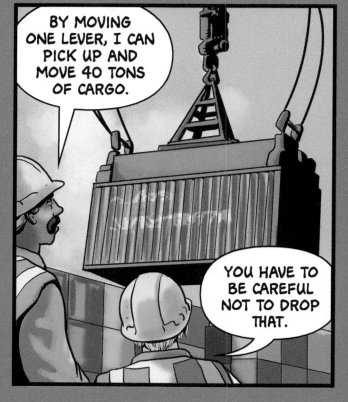

A BUSY PORT HAS LOTS OF WORKERS. THEY MOVE AND STORE GOODS.

LET'S GET OUT OF THE WAY, BRIANNA.

WE'LL TALK TO SAM WHEN HE'S IN THE CRANE.

YOU MADE IT! HOW HIGH UP ARE YOU, SAM?

ABOUT 140 FEET. I'LL SEND A PICTURE TO SHOW YOU THE INSIDE.

WHAT ARE ALL THOSE LIGHTS?

THEY HELP ME KNOW WHEN IT'S SAFE TO PICK UP AND THEN DROP OFF A CONTAINER.

AFTER CONTAINERS COME OFF THE SHIP, THEY ARE PLACED IN A CONTAINER YARD.

TRUCKS AND TRAINS MOVE GOODS FROM THE PORTS TO PLACES ALL OVER THE UNITED STATES.

SAM'S JOB LOOKS EASY, BUT IT'S NOT.

I THINK IT LOOKS LIKE FUN!

ART: EUREKA COMICS

67

YOU GOT TO MOVE IT!

SHIPS IN, SHIPS OUT

Do you know where your bananas come from? You might think they come from California. After all, California grows so many fruits! But most bananas are **imported** from other countries. The last banana you ate probably came through one of California's shipping ports. Every day, tons of goods are imported and **exported**, or sent to other countries, through ports. In 2015, over 15 million 20-foot containers moved through ports in California.

TRAINS AND TRUCKS

Goods don't move just by ship in the United States. Huge amounts of products are transported across the country on trains and trucks. In fact, more than 49 million tons of goods are moved on trucks and trains each day. That's a lot of stuff!

WordBlast

What does the word **export** mean? If *import* is the opposite of *export*, what does **import** mean?

Bananas are unloaded from ships and into trucks.

Truck drivers move goods across the country.

TRANSPORTATION

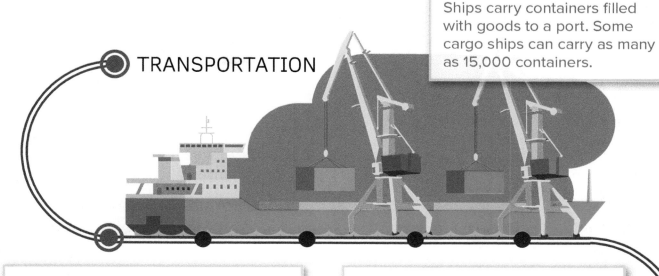

Ships carry containers filled with goods to a port. Some cargo ships can carry as many as 15,000 containers.

Trains and trucks transport the goods across the country. Some goods travel in the shipping containers.

A train can carry up to 200 containers. Trucks can move goods in or out of a shipping container.

Workers unload the goods. Trucks of all different sizes deliver them to stores close to where you live.

STORE

 EXPLORE the InfoGraphic

- How many containers can a big cargo ship carry?
- How many containers can a train carry?
- Explain how a TV might move from China to a store near you.

CALIFORNIA KIDS HELP

REINS IN MOTION

Kids really can make a difference! Just ask the volunteers at Reins in Motion. It's a horseback-riding program in Livermore, California. People with disabilities learn to ride horses with the help of a teacher.

Students at a local middle school came to the rescue when the riding program needed a ramp for wheelchairs. They sold cups of hot chocolate, and in a week, they raised $300, enough to build the ramp. Now it's easier for riders to get on the horses. And it's all thanks to kids willing to help their community.

Reins in Motion and other groups like the one in the picture help people with disabilities learn to ride horses.

Tina Stallard/The Image Bank/Getty Images

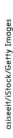

IZZY'S CORNER

In California, hundreds of thousands of people don't have enough food to eat. Izzy's Corner is part of a food bank in Orange County. Here, kids help other kids. Volunteers come one day a week to pack food. Then they distribute it to families in the area. At Izzy's Corner, small acts of kindness make a big difference.

HOW KIDS CAN HELP

Do you want to help your community, too? There are plenty of ways. These are just a few ideas. You might have some of your own!

- **Visit a** senior center. You can sing songs or read books together.

- **Volunteer** at an animal shelter. Maybe you can walk dogs.

- **Raise money** for a charity you care about. Organize a bake sale or a penny drive.

- **Sort cans** at a food bank, or plan a food drive to bring in donations.

- **Clean up** a park or a beach. Keep your community clean and safe.

IF IT DID GROW ON TREES

by **Betsy Hebert**

Money, they say,
Doesn't grow on trees.

But what if it did?
What if the tree in my yard
Had dollar bills for leaves?

I would water that money tree
Every day, every night!
It would grow and grow.

I'd pick money any time.
New shoes, new games,
New every single thing I want.

Hmm.

And then what?

OlegErin/iStock/Getty Images

Take Action!

More to Explore

What else would you like to know about? The questions below have more ideas for you to research and discuss.

What crops are grown in California?

Where do they go?

How can you volunteer in your community?

How much solar power does the United States use?

WordBlast

- Why does a country **export** goods?
- Why does a country **import** goods?
- What are your favorite kinds of **produce** to eat?
- Name two **sources** of energy we use today.

Reflect

How do people in a community meet their needs?

What Do I Say?

....

Here are some ways you can talk with a partner or a small group.

Remember to . . .

Ask questions that add to the conversation.

- Why do you think the author said this?
- Why do you think that? Tell me more.
- I'm confused by . . . .

Why do you think that?

Christopher Futcher/E+/Getty Images

Can you explain?

Connect ideas to other texts or situations.

- This reminds me of what we learned in . . . .
- This is a lot like . . . .
- This makes me think about . . . .

Help your partner explain more.

- Do you mean that . . . ?
- Can you explain that?
- Can you give me more examples?

Talk about what your partner said earlier.

- What you said made me think about . . . .
- I'd like to add to what you just said.
- I want to go back to what you said before.

Challenge an idea.

- Where in the text did you find that evidence?
- Show me where the author says that.
- How do you know that?

Clear up misunderstandings.

- Okay, so what you're saying is . . . .
- What do you mean by . . . ?
- I'm not sure I know what you mean. Can you explain?

Disagree politely.

- I hear what you're saying. I also think that . . . .
- I'm not so sure. Maybe . . . .
- I see it differently.

Support your ideas with examples.

- In the text it says that . . . .
- For example . . . .
- The reason I think this is because . . . .

This is a lot like . . . .

WordBlast

A

activist
a person who uses action to make change

D

debris
the remains of something that has been damaged or broken down

decompose
to break down, rot, or decay

destination
a place reached at the end of a journey

E

exclude
to keep someone or something out

export
to send goods to another country

I

import
to bring goods in from another country

industry
a business that provides a certain kind of good or service

M

mimic
to copy or imitate

P

population
the number of people, animals, or plants living in a place

preserve
to keep safe or protect

prevent
to stop something from happening

produce
fruits and vegetables grown by a farmer

R

regalia
special clothing, usually worn for important occasions

repeal
to end or do away with something

reservoir
a place to store liquids, such as a lake to store water

rodeo
a show or display of cowboy skills

S

source
the place or thing from which something comes

T

traditional
relating to customs that have been in place for a long time

transform
to change completely